WISDOM
ON THE WAY TO
WALL STREET

WISDOM
ON THE WAY TO
WALL STREET

22
Steps to Navigate Your Road To Success

MATTHEW C. MEADE

DEDICATION

To my family -

I am here not by my own strength but through the collective strength of the people who have helped carry me thus far -- God, my mother, my family, the students I have encouraged from different schools, my colleagues, professors, teachers, mentors and friends. With all of my heart, THANK YOU for finding me worthy enough to be supported and loved. You are all instruments of God's continuous presence in my life. I hope to make you very proud one day and continue to push the legacy forward.

Matthew C. Meade

YOUR ROAD MAP

CHAPTER 1

You are the CEO of your own life

Some of the most powerful businessmen and businesswomen began their road to a life of success by living ordinary lives doing ordinary things. Jeff Bezos, for example, worked as a line-cook at his local McDonalds. He later became the founder of Amazon, Inc. Steve Jobs was an introvert throughout school and often isolated himself. Focusing on his master plan, he later founded Apple, Inc., which grew to become one of the largest technology companies of all time. Shawn "Jay-Z" Carter grew up in the streets of Brooklyn from humble beginnings and later became a businessman and is now the fifth black billionaire in the United States of America. These individuals have made a tremendous impact on the world we live in today simply because they did not let their past affect their future.

You may be asking yourself "this is how they started but what does that have to do with where I am now?" To answer that question, I'm going to use the example of a thriving business or company. As a Chief Executive Officer (CEO) you are in charge of all aspects of a company. You may have hundreds or thousands of people who work for you and report to you but when it comes to all decisions, you have the final say. You may delegate tasks or responsibilities to other people but again, the CEO makes the final decision based on their knowledge, experiences, and following their intuition. There may be times when the person in charge has to be quick on their feet and make decisions without having all of the facts, background or information to support it. In these situations they have to take risks, chances, and trust their gut feeling. These are the times when you have to carefully assess what you know and learn lessons from what you don't know. You make the final decisions and those decisions directly affect your progress for better or for worse. But always remember you are the CEO of your own life. You run the business of you and have the power to make the decisions necessary to drive your success regardless of where you began.

Like a startup company, you at times have to make decisions quickly, fail fast, and embrace the unknown. Not every decision you make will be the right choice but you can't win the game if you don't attempt to score. Similar to Steve Jobs, Jeff Bezos and Shawn Carter, make sure that you are making executive decisions that will propel you from humble beginnings to a platform that outlives you.

CHAPTER 2

Embrace the audacity to be authentically you

We live in a world where it's easy to follow a trend or the majority but you have to be true to yourself and embrace the audacity to be authentically you. In life, you will work in many teams whether it's through extracurricular activities, school, or your job. Knowing yourself is essential to becoming a great leader and adding meaningful contributions when working in groups. Just as important as it is to know who you are, it's also important to know who you are not. When working in teams it is good for each person to know what they bring to the table. On the best teams in competitive sports, each player knows and operates in their strengths and relies on others in the areas of their short-comings. This allows everyone to help benefit the team as a whole. Take Michael Jordan, Scottie Pippen, and Dennis Rodman of the Chicago Bulls for example. This trio is known for being one of the NBA's greatest dynasties, winning six NBA Championships between 1991 and 1998. When on the court, each player complimented each other because they played towards their strengths and knew their weaknesses. Rodman was good at defense while Jordan and Pippen were good at shooting. The trio wouldn't have worked at the same level if each member of the team wasn't aware of their individual strengths and weaknesses and knew what the team needed them to contribute.

The pop band, The Jonas Brothers, consists of brothers Kevin, Joe, and Nick. Each member has a unique sound and performance style that contributes to their overall music success in developing chart topping records and reaching their fan base. After releasing five albums, the band decided to part ways with each member going on to pursue their individual musical crafts. A few years later, the band rejoined to answer the call of their fans and released an album that again topped the charts. As independent artists the brothers had moderate success and notoriety but as a collective unit, they were able to reach a level that exceeded expectations. This goes to show that everyone playing their instrument together and playing it well is when you create timeless music.

When doing business, like playing sports competitively, you never want to compromise your ethics or integrity. Sometimes circumstances will be challenging but you should never change your character or the principles which define you. The components that make you authentic should not change based on external circumstances. Doing the right thing is contagious and good people will be drawn to you as you proceed on a positive path. If you see yourself on a negative track remember that can always be changed in a positive direction but it's vital to have the proper viewpoint that things will work in your favor. Whether they are good or bad in its present state you have to own the mindset that it's working for you and not against you. Your attitude towards the circumstances sets the tone for the outcome. In order to transform the path you are on you have to be willing to make the change.

As you are meeting new people and developing new relationships you should always go where you're celebrated and not simply tolerated. You must know your worth because people will give you what you will tolerate. Personally, I have always tried to be the best version of myself, especially in situations or rooms where no one looked like me. Throughout school and working in finance there were often times where I was the only black male in the room. As a result, the diversity I would bring by being my authentic self, added a unique perspective to the conversations.

I can recall a time when I worked at an organization where there was an initiative to help increase financial literacy within the black community by targeting African-American women. The organization hosted events for black women to attend and learn from financial professionals about investment best practices and the importance of economic empowerment. Although the event was targeting women, as a black male I attended not just to support the mission but to also provide insight from a different perspective. Think about it like this, no one can be the best version of you except you. We were all made differently. When you're being the best authentic version of you, you're making your personal mark on the world and creating an opportunity for someone else to learn something new.

CHAPTER 3

Blaze your own trail

"Don't go where the path may lead, go instead where there is no path and leave a trail."

- Ralph Waldo Emerson

Michael Phelps, one of the greatest Olympic athletes in history has admirable skill and ability. One of the key components that contributes to Michael's success is his focus on himself, the race before him and staying in his own lane. You have to blaze your own trail. In order to do this, you have to be flexible in trying different things that have never been done before. You might surprise yourself at what you are naturally good at when you step outside of the box and be open minded enough to try new and different things. Do what makes you happy instead of what everyone else is doing or expects you to do. If you're in a career that makes you happy you'll never work a day in your life. This is not easy to find but if you are aware of it now you certainly can begin the search. The search is the adventure. It's an opportunity to try new things even if they seem outlandish or are outside of your comfort zone. Once you find what you love it's essential to follow and flourish in your passion. You need to know your passion and expertise so then people can know you for the viewpoint you can add. As a result, when others order from the menu make sure your expertise ends up on the table. With a heightened level of passion you will differentiate yourself putting you on the road to success.

Within your journey it's crucial to bet on yourself. No one is going to believe in you unless you believe in yourself. Most people don't want to be a part of something unproductive or something that may sound unrealistic. They want to be a part of positivity and evolution. If you have an idea, it's better to spend time developing it, creating something that people can physically touch or visualize in their mind because you've spent the time crafting it. This shows people that you have invested in your idea and you are not just talking about what you're going to do. Then when you present it to investors or other people, they too can see your vision and believe in it and therefore are more likely to want to help you take it to the next level. Once you bet on you and create something that's beneficial to society, you'll be astounded by how people will reach out to you and look to find ways to be a part of your endeavor.

I want you to leave it all on the table. No matter what you build or the trail you ignite, be the best at it. Look to be number one in your field, the person that people can go to and count on. You don't want to be average, we were never put on this Earth to be average. We are expected to be the head and not the tail and stand out amongst the pack.

Always remember, the energy you put out in the world is the same energy you will get back. Putting out positive energy attracts like-minded people to you. Alternatively, putting out negative energy will connect you to negative people and may put you in tough circumstances. I can remember friends that I grew up with who always did well in school, got great internships and are now flourishing in their careers. Some have even built inspirational startups or nonprofit organizations. I have other friends who I grew up with that were easily influenced and followed the wrong crowds. As a result, they had a more difficult time in school and would often end up either in the legal system or passing away early due to criminal activity. It's not a direct correlation but once you get stuck in the system it's challenging to pull yourself out of that situation. It's possible, but challenging.

I always tell people when you are blazing your own trail you will face challenges and opposition but expect to win. When you differentiate yourself opportunities will arise. When they do, know that it's because of the work you did to set yourself apart. When you find yourself in a business meeting or a job interview it's because you're supposed to be there. Sometimes when doors start to open, we tend to think we are not enough. Once you get in the room make sure to capitalize on your moment. Embrace the purpose because opportunities will present themselves if you work long and hard enough and when they do, walk in like a champion. You have to know you will win but the capacity of how you win is often correlated with the size of the risks you take in venturing off from the crowd. Big risks may lead to big rewards but that doesn't often come from a place of comfort.

CHAPTER 4

Get comfortable being uncomfortable

We can always strive to plan and prepare to the best of our ability but you may find yourself at times in situations that are not always ideal or comfortable. A vital part of growth and developing endurance is to get comfortable with being uncomfortable. The biggest opportunities for growth can be discovered when you are doing something outside of your comfort zone. When you're too comfortable it's easy to become stagnant. This is a dangerous place to be. You should want to grow in all aspects of life. Consistently strive to be the best version of yourself and aim for opportunities to grow. When you're constantly trying to better yourself, doors will open for you that you couldn't have even dreamed of. Your brand is how people perceive you based on the reputation of your work. Take a chance on something new but make sure it's on the course towards your end goal. This requires sacrifice which is a prerequisite to growth and building your craft, relationships, and brand. Not all open doors are meant to be walked through. The wrong door can easily dilute or destroy your brand. Always assess whether the door opened is right for you.

I can recall times in my career where I changed jobs, firms or careers and wasn't really sure if I made the right decision. In these situations I took a leap of faith and knew that if I was considered for the role that I was the best candidate for it. I was able to try many different fields through internships and school helped me to understand what I liked and disliked. I've declined jobs that paid more if they weren't on my path towards my end goal to being an Executive. In the end the underlying principle I learned was that uncertainty has realized gains. Some of the gains that I experienced were growth, adaptability to different situations, meeting diverse people and learning alternative leadership styles and most of all, learning about myself.

Consider a goalie on a soccer team. I remember growing up playing soccer the goalie had one of the hardest jobs on the field. Not only do they have to protect the team's net but also have to play defense at times. In order to play defense though, the goalie has to step away from the net to join with the rest of the team. In stepping away from the net, they are essentially leaving the net susceptible to being scored on. This is an uncomfortable situation and requires a lot of skill. When handled correctly by assessing the situation on the field first and checking for the placement of the opposing team, the right opportunity may arise for the goalie to make a tremendous impact. Like the goalie, when the opportunity presents itself don't be afraid to step away from your comfort zone and take risks as you navigate your path.

CHAPTER 5

Dare to take risks

Taking risks is a necessary part of obtaining success. We know that being comfortable or complacent can negatively affect your growth. You have to dare to take risks but don't just take the first step, take a leap of faith in all that you do. Pursue your wildest dreams and never let anyone tell you that you cannot do something. In your leap of faith there will be unexpected obstacles thrown your way. The unexpected hurdles will test your faith in how much you want the dream to come to fruition. In these cases it's always beneficial to have a support network that reminds you of the opportunities versus the risks associated with what you are striving to do. This network can be heavily relied on in times of doubt. You should never doubt yourself, but sometimes when things are taking longer than expected to occur you may question it, but your faith has to be greater than your fears. Not only do you need strong faith, you must have long faith.

When taking risks you have to be bold. If you want what is meant for you, boldness is a prerequisite because taking risks won't get easier over time but tolerance increases with each risk you overcome. Remember, fortune goes to the bold. The more risks you take the more adaptable you are to certain situations because you have developed experience. If you're not willing to risk the usual you'll have to settle for the ordinary. No one should want to be ordinary, we were all uniquely made to reach significant potential. I have taken risks whether it was starting a new job, moving locations, or investment endeavors. One difficult thing about taking these risks was uncertainty. I would keep good people around me for coaching and advice but most importantly I was faithful that the task at hand would be successful.

One risk I have taken was directly emailing the CEO of JP Morgan Chase & Company (JPM) requesting to join the firm by emphasizing the value I would add to the business. He was speaking at an event that I attended for a non-profit organization and encouraged anyone in the audience who felt qualified to be a part of the organization to email him directly. As a result, that's what I did five years later. I started working at JPM a year after that. I don't know if the result was a direct correlation but either way, I was willing to take him up on his offer. As you take risks it'll be uncomfortable at times but as a leader you have to tap into that feeling of discomfort and use it as your fuel towards realizing your full potential. Either you can dare to take risks or risk living a life of mediocrity.

CHAPTER 6

Know your strengths overcome your weaknesses

At all times you should know your strengths, but more importantly understand and strive to overcome your weaknesses. When you are aware of the areas where you struggle you can then tackle those areas with the help of others who are knowledgeable in that area. Always do your own due diligence to have basic fundamental understanding first so that way when you ask for help you'll be able to communicate your specific needs. Being honest and open to acknowledging your weaknesses is a sign of strength and vulnerability. People will want to help you learn and improve by owning and being aware of your shortcomings.

For me personally, I've always been good at interacting with people, strategizing, analyzing information and building businesses. As a result, in jobs and working with people I tend to look to use some of these traits to add the most value to the team. However, one thing that I'm not as good at is programming.

Therefore, I recognize when I need external resources and hire someone in that expertise. However, I continue to learn in order to make that weakness a strength. Another example of someone who overcame their weaknesses and capitalized on their strengths is Tim Tebow. Tim was a recipient of the Heisman Trophy. He then went on to play in the National Football League. After being traded and experiencing a decrease in playing time, Tim changed his trajectory and pursued a career in professional baseball. He took full advantage of his wide-range of skills and made it work for him instead of against him.

Lastly, it's important to continue to develop your abilities because they too can easily become shortcomings if you aren't careful. You don't want to get ahead of yourself and neglect the areas where you are efficient so much that they become weaknesses over time. For me, math was a subject that always came easy in school but I struggled in history due to the memorization. As a result, I would continue to develop in math and look to focus more on history until it became more intuitive. Thus my standardized test scores in both subjects improved. This thought process is also helpful in knowing your expertise as you're elevating towards your purpose.

CHAPTER 7

Your elevation may require isolation

t's always good to have supporters in your corner although sometimes your elevation may require isolation from family members and friends. Not any and everyone is meant to walk your path with you. Each year I review my contacts and see who still is on the same path as me or who I should no longer associate with. It may sound weird but it's necessary to know who your friends are and who your friends aren't. Yes, I know, those people are in your circle but are they in your corner? You have to constantly ask yourself this question as you assess your friendships and if you do it correctly as you grow your circle should get smaller. Think about it like coin currency, specifically the comparison of a nickel to a dime. A dime is much smaller in size compared to a nickel. However, a dime holds more value than the nickel. Your relationships should be viewed in the same light. The smaller group of friends you surround yourself with should hold more weight to you than being associated with a larger group of people.

In elementary school I was one of the South Mountain Superstars which is a kid that did well in school and was a popular leader amongst the students. In middle school, I was best dressed in the yearbook, played basketball and was very popular amongst my peers. In high school, I won homecoming king and was captain of the basketball and soccer teams. Today, I speak consistently to five people out of the large circles I was once associated with. It really came down to who was an asset and who was a liability. Think for a minute who genuinely wants to see you progress into a better person and who really wants to see you win. Alternatively, who only takes from you and may not necessarily want what's best for you. These are the people you have to remove yourself from in order to reach the next level. The most important thing you can do on your road to expansion is protect your energy. If you do that well, you will attract positivity and negate negativity.

When you're working in your quiet space and focusing on leveling up, everyone doesn't need to know what your next move is going to be. Focus on the task at hand and let the results be your noise. Oftentimes living in a society based on social media people post everything they are doing online for others to like and comment. Outside opinions are not necessary when you are working in your own lane and trying to elevate. When you're in the space of growth, creativity and innovation it's best to work more and talk less. You'll get more done focusing on and mastering your craft and gain a clearer vision on what you want to manifest.

CHAPTER 8

Master your craft

A sculptor doesn't create masterpieces overnight. It takes years and years of practice to master the craft of creating something spectacular. When you're doing an activity and actually enjoy it so much that it doesn't feel like work, that is your passion and your passion will lead you to your purpose. Invest your time in what excites you or makes you feel most alive. One of the easiest ways to find out what you're good at is by taking a wide range of classes in school. The subjects that you do well in and come easier to you could give you a good indication of your purpose. I've always been good with numbers and once I did an internship in finance I knew that I should pursue investment banking. I'm an outgoing person that always enjoys interacting with people so the first job I took was in capital market sales. In this space I would interact with clients but also be able to use my market knowledge and technical skills to build models. This role was a great fit for my background. Assess what you're passionate about and hone in on those skills to make a greater impact for yourself and others.

As you're creating something great stay in your lane and focus on the mission ahead, but don't be afraid to break down barriers. There may be people who have already traveled the road that you are pursuing. You should always acknowledge and know when you need to ask for help. As mentioned previously, acknowledging your weaknesses is a sign of strength that people will respect you for. Develop a relationship with people who have paved the way and look for ways to learn from them. Don't let anyone or anything stop you from mastering your craft.

When mastering your craft there are no shortcuts on the road to greatness. Many want to be great but don't want to put in the work or make the sacrifices. It could take 10,000+ hours of preparation and practice to master your craft. You can't cut corners and your highest level of attention is needed. From time to time I would hear about so-called "get rich quick" schemes some of which were often illegal so I never invested time or resources into them. You don't want to get caught in something where you are looking to make money fast but not sure about the validity of the venture. Always do your research and if it doesn't feel or seem right, it probably isn't. The success of the strongest and well known businesses didn't happen overnight. It takes several years of hard work, adaptability, and education to create a sustainable product. Tesla, Inc. is one of the leading makers of luxury, electric cars. Initially, Tesla encountered several issues gaining traction in the automobile market. The lack of outlets available for drivers to charge their vehicles was one of the hurdles that had to be addressed. Not to mention, this occurred in a time period where electric cars were still considered futuristic. Tesla did not begin to truly see a demand and gain their footprint in the market until almost ten years later. This goes to show that it can take significant time to see the return on your investment of energy and effort.

CHAPTER 9

Endlessly educate yourself

In order to keep yourself competitive in today's environment you must never stop learning. The capacity to learn something new is endless. There are opportunities to expose yourself to new things through school, reading books, listening to podcasts, traveling, meeting new people or even daily conversations. Once you stop growing and educating yourself it's time to change what you are doing. If you're in a job for a while and you feel like you're no longer being challenged don't hesitate to start looking for the next suitable role for your growth. I take advantage of every chance I get to understand something new because the information that can be obtained is immeasurable. A great way to constantly educate yourself is to read. Whether you are reading an article a day or a book a month, you can learn something new from reading.

I spent four years of high school working hard, studying, and earning good grades my top priority over social activities. Endlessly educating myself reaped major rewards when I received a full academic scholarship to attend the University of Virginia.

After I graduated, I began working in finance in New York City. Thirteen years after crossing the stage, I decided to pick up my backpack again to pursue my Executive MBA.

The times I look back and reflect on where I learned many important principles were through sports and other extracurricular activities. Through playing basketball I learned the importance of teamwork, time management, leadership, drive and dedication. These principles, along with good character and integrity, I am able to apply daily on Wall Street within teams and working with colleagues. Furthermore, the principles of doing what you say you're going to do, being your authentic self and putting your best foot forward establishes a reputable reputation.

The main thing I want you to know is that knowledge is power. The more knowledge you have the easier it is to make sound decisions. In school you're taught a lesson and then given a test. In life, you are given a test that teaches you a lesson. As a result, if you have the knowledge beforehand those lessons won't set you back and moving forward in your journey can become much easier.

CHAPTER 10

Rebound to foster resilience

Nothing is more frustrating than when you are driving to a destination and you continuously run into red lights along the way. You're sitting behind the steering wheel and as the next intersection approaches you're anxious for a long awaited green light. Similarly, I have run into many red lights while pursuing my aspirations and have been told "no" so many times whether applying to opportunities or trying new things. Oftentimes you'll see people try to put you in a box for who they think you are or should be. It's important to break down those walls and be who you know you are and not who people expect you to be. You may be told no or turned down for an opportunity but you owe it to yourself to never give up. A "no" today can be a "yes" tomorrow.

There are many notable individuals who were able to master the ability to fail forward. Oprah Winfrey is a great example as she was fired from her first job as an on air personality. She later went on to start the famous Oprah Winfrey Show which aired for 25 seasons. Michael Jordan was cut from his high school basketball team. He once said, "I have missed over 9,000 shots in my career. I have lost almost 300 games. On 26 occasions I have been entrusted to take the game winning shot, and I have missed. I have failed over and over and over again in my life and that is why I succeed." Even Barack Obama, who before becoming the 44th and the first black President of the United States of America, lost an election in 2000 to represent Illinois in the U.S. House of Representatives.

You have to accept the fact that at times, you will be turned down. People may not initially believe in your idea but if you continue to believe in yourself and work hard, they will eventually see your vision unfold. Don't get held up by what people say or think. I turn rejection into my motivation to keep propelling forward.

The brightest ideas can emerge from the darkest places. As you're being told no or rejected, bounce back even stronger. Sometimes being told "no" can be a blessing in disguise for something far greater to come in the future. Make sure to outlast the rejection because your ability to be triumphant does not diminish based on how others view you. Don't let walls be built around who you are or your capabilities. Remember that rejection and being dismissed is a collateral experience of having the audacity to be yourself. In a strange way it is a confirmation and affirmation of your journey down your own path. Limitations can come from how other people view you but it can also come from internally within yourself. Thoughts become things. What you think can easily become your reality. Negativity is contagious but so is positivity. This is often called The Law of Attraction. You have to view yourself as a triumphant leader that works to get things done in a positive way. If you don't view yourself in this light, others won't view you in this light either. If you think to yourself that you cannot do something or it will not happen, it probably won't. However, if your thoughts about yourself are victorious and you come up slightly short of your goal you are still guaranteed a chance to build resilience as you bounce back.

Turn your losses into lessons. I can recall a time when I lost a significant amount of money on a bad real estate investment deal. I had two choices at that point: the first was to give up, stay depressed and bitter about the choice I made. The second was to accept the bad decision, put it behind me, bounce back and try to do better the next time. While it was a really tough experience for me to feel like I messed up and failed, in the end it made me much stronger in character, appreciative of what I have and much smarter in making investment deals. In this situation, I accepted the bad decision as a lesson and continued looking ahead for better opportunities that I knew were soon to come.

Keep moving in the direction of progression

Time waits for no one. The clock never stops ticking. Each year, month, week, day, hour, minute and second you will never get back. Similar to time, don't live in the past, keep moving forward. Only look back to reflect on your journey and see how far you've come. Life is extremely short so we must keep moving ahead and learn from the lessons acquired along the way. I look at every situation as a blessing or a lesson. If it's a positive situation, then it was a blessing that I was fortunate enough to have the experience. However, if it was a negative situation, then it was an opportunity for me to learn something new or take something away from it. Growing up was a tough experience but a rewarding one. I grew up in a family of five brothers and two sisters. We were all very close and still are. My mother worked tirelessly to instill values in us like strong work ethic, focusing on your craft, being a good servant and valuing others. She encouraged us to work hard to not only get into college but to graduate and make a better future for ourselves. She said, "Work hard in school to open up doors because nothing is given to you. You have to create opportunities for yourself."

My father passed away when I was ten years old. It was a difficult situation for me to understand and adapt to at such a young age. As a result, I would often lean on my older brothers or mentors for advice in certain situations. I could have taken this situation and let it break me down but instead I went through the emotions of the situation and adapted to this change. It was the first time that I ever experienced a death and for it to be a parent was an enormous pill to swallow for a young person. However, I learned that God will never put more on me than I can bare and the same goes for you. No one lives in physical form forever so we have to live each day on this Earth trying to be a better person than we were the day before and show the people close to us how much we love and appreciate them.

As I began to work hard and discover who I wanted to be, I had to remember to celebrate the small wins. Sometimes we can get so bogged down with working to achieve what's next that we forget to acknowledge and celebrate our accomplishments. It's also good to pause and level set on the lessons learned so far. There is no win too small to celebrate. Some people wait until others celebrate their accomplishments and while that is great, please don't forget to celebrate yourself and to celebrate each step in your journey, big or small.

I really want to highlight everything you want is on the other side of fear. Sometimes the task we have in front of us can be so big we don't know where to start. Fear and hesitancy can immobilize us but pushing forward will help you to knock down that wall piece by piece. If you never start you will always lose. You have to start somewhere and oftentimes it will not play out as you planned but in the long run the overall goal will be accomplished. It's tough at times to face your fears but if you approach it with the proper mindset, the will to take risks and determination you should be able to overcome the obstacles. There will be hurdles but you have to be a version of yourself that will not accept defeat. Make sure to move forward with purpose.

CHAPTER 12

Your next level demands a different you

As you get older and progress from stage to stage, each phase will demand a different you. You have to blaze your own trail, get comfortable with being uncomfortable, and dare to take risks. If you keep doing the same actions you will garner the same results. The results obtained will reflect the work you put into the task. If you don't study for a test you can't expect to perform well. You have to prepare and position yourself to be successful. When facing trials and tribulations, always keep in mind that to whom much is given much is required. I like to say "don't complain about how much you have on your plate if you came to eat." As long as you're working hard and delivering results with high integrity, opportunities will come your way. As you have spent the time mastering your craft, expect to see the fruits of your labor.

To maximize your potential you can't be who you were

yesterday. You'll have to break down old, bad habits to make room for new, good habits. One of the habits that I recently developed was eating healthier. Before I would always eat fast food because it was cheap and convenient. As I started to eat healthier my body felt better, I was able to think clearer, became more productive and in better shape. Furthermore, I started going to sleep a little earlier each night to wake up early in the morning to work on different passion projects. I've been doing this for the last year and it quickly became one of my most productive years. Developing good habits such as being polite, grateful, respectful, dependable, consistent, on time and operating with high integrity will open doors for you. Try to be aware of bad habits and once you recognize them, remove them from your regular routine. Shake the bad habits and expand upon the good ones to be great. Life is a transformative process and each day is a new opportunity to reinvent yourself.

While you are growing and transforming don't lose who you are at your core in the process of reaching the next level. Always be true to yourself and don't compromise your values or what you stand for in any circumstance. Stand on the principles that define you. Make sure you are the same person when no one's watching you. Don't be a people pleaser by trying to be someone you are not just to be liked or accepted. Be your same self to everyone. Always remember you rent your title but own your character. That's right, you rent your title but own your character. You will progress within your career but the mental and moral qualities distinctive to you should not change. Having good character is a vital aspect to building your brand and being successful.

CHAPTER 13

Persevere with spirituality

The road can be difficult at times and you may question what your purpose is. During these times you have to believe in yourself as well as something greater than you. For me, that something greater is Jesus Christ, the Great I Am. He has pulled me through the most trying times I've encountered. What I learned is that you have to have unshakeable faith. Storms will arise with strong winds that threaten to knock you down. However, like a palm tree, which bends and moves in a hurricane, you have to withstand the storm. You will bend at times as it is a part of the growing process but you won't be broken and what doesn't kill you, only makes you stronger. If you don't have solid faith the enemy can try to trick you or interfere with your progress. It's important to know who the enemy is, who he uses and his tactics like depression or doubt to knock you off your path. The enemy can come at you in many ways but it's on you to stay woke and be aware of his presence and schemes. The enemy often comes as a wolf in sheep's clothing. When you know who your enemy is, you then have the ability to arm yourself for what is to come and trust me, IT WILL come. Most importantly you should be prepared with what you need to be most successful which is faith and prayer. Be mindful though that at times you can become your own worst enemy. This is when being the CEO of your own life and being your number one fan, supporter, and cheerleader solidifies your self-determination to coach yourself to success.

When persevering with spirituality you have to accept what is, let go of what was and have faith in what is to become. Everything happens for a reason. You cannot erase the past. If you are ashamed of certain experiences in the past use them as learning lessons. Your hands should be so busy catching blessings that you don't have any capacity to hold onto grudges. Forgive and let negative things go so you can make room for the new blessings coming your way. I remember when I sold one of my old houses and moved. I had a storage bin with lots of older belongings that I didn't necessarily need but was holding onto. Once I moved into my new home I ended up giving stuff away to those in need and at the same time was able to make room to add to my new environment. The same principle should be applied to your experiences. Recognize experiences for what they were but for the bad ones learn from them and let them go. It is almost impossible to move forward if you keep replaying the past. Use the past as memories, learning lessons and moments to propel you forward.

Lastly, I want you to know that faith in action is a prerequisite to manifestation. When you have hope and faith in what is to come, it will manifest. Let me be clear, dreams only work if you do. If you are faithful about becoming a business owner and getting an investment to start your business you will have to have a business plan, network and meet with potential investors for it to happen. If you always wanted to be a restaurant owner you should try different foods, research locations and be able to provide a high level of customer service for it to be successful. You have to work towards what you're praying for to have it manifest. Sometimes just you and your higher power have to go on the journey alone for you to reach your full potential. In these times, prayer is your number one tool to get you through. Spending time talking to God is an act of your faith in Him. It shows that you are not just relying on your abilities but also in His and you are actively inviting Him into the situation. With God involved, there is absolutely no way you can fail but trying to make something happen without him is a recipe for disaster. You have to work alongside Him. God will open doors for you but you have to take the step and walk through them. I advise you to often pause and pray at different steps in your endeavor. Make prayer a constant practice to remain in fellowship with Him and ensure that you are on the right path which should always be His path. Knowing who you are and having a solid relationship with God gives you a light that shines for others to see, attracts people to you and gives you the ability to bring others to know Him.

CHAPTER 14

Build your board of directors

mentioned previously that you are the CEO of your own life. Every CEO has to have a strong Board of Directors. The Board serves as the people who come together, strategize, and vote on the best and innovative ideas to help the business succeed. For personal and professional progression you want to ensure that your Board has the same positive traits that you see within yourself. Recognize influential people who are where you are striving to be. These people are leaders who have paved the way in the area that you are pursuing. You can look to them for advice as you face challenges on your journey. As you are taking advice, keep in mind that all advice is not great advice. You have to apply it to your situation and see what works best for you. Establishing strong mentors can help you with decision making and avoiding mistakes so you can reach your final goal with less hurdles. I have five people on my board of directors that I look to for advice. These people have been working in different industries, have a wide range of experiences and are very seasoned within their professions.

As you prepare for discussions with your board members make sure you equip yourself for the meeting. Preparation is very important. Always understand your objective and goal for scheduling a meeting. Mentors are very busy and could be doing many other things outside of meeting with you. Therefore, when you request a meeting be over prepared, know why you're hosting the meeting, have an agenda and be on time. Show respect for the time allocated by the individual and keep topics on the agenda so you don't go over the scheduled time. During the meeting listen more and talk less. It's difficult to listen and learn if you are constantly talking. Once the meeting is over, send the meeting minutes (notes) and don't forget to do the appropriate follow-up action items. This separates an average mentee from one that is passionate and engaged to be helped on their journey to success.

We are designed as humans to be in fellowship with others. We all need people. In order to broaden your circle of influence, you must network with positive peers. I can't emphasize enough the importance of avoiding negative people. You must surround yourself with people who see greatness and positivity in all situations. There are some people that wake up in the morning and if they miss their train or spill their coffee, they instantly feel like their entire day is ruined. It's important to see and expect positivity in not just situations, but also in the people you surround yourself with. The people you surround yourself with should be so positive and focused on their goals and supporting yours that they know that if you win, everyone wins and if they win, everyone wins. We all have a seat at the table. You can either get there alone or you can have a support group to navigate your way to the top. It's like the saying goes, "It takes a village to raise a child." The same goes for your passion. Don't try to get to the top on your own. Even if you are the Michael Jordan of your brand, remember the Chicago Bulls of the 1990's were a success because of teamwork and reliance on each other. You, as CEO, are no different in building your own dynasty.

If you surround yourself with winners you have a much stronger probability to win too. Your weakest link in your circle can weigh down everyone's progress. If you look at your closest five friends, you should not be the most intelligent in the group. If that's the case you will need to make changes to your group of friends. You want to empower your people but make sure you are surrounding yourself with forward thinking individuals. With diverse perspectives everyone has something to offer and at the same token everyone has something to learn. It's essential to have these people around you to brainstorm ideas and celebrate wins and losses with. My closest relationships are people who I have known since middle and high school. We built our relationships over the years from humble beginnings, common interest and the will to win. This collection of friends have positive energy, operate with high integrity and truly want the best for each other.

CHAPTER 15

Illustrate your perception through integrity

You want to be known and viewed as someone who operates with integrity. It's good to be someone people can count on which is a result of delivering on your promises. To build your brand as a reliable individual, your word is everything. What has really helped me with career progression was delivering on what I said I would do. You should exhibit honor, morals and good ethics. Protect your name and brand with all that you have. I can recall times where in the news there would be people who worked their entire career to build a reputable image. Then after one bad encounter with the law or a momentary lapse of judgement, everything they worked for was ruined. A short gain is never worth the time it takes to rebrand yourself. Make sure to be authentic and operate with great character because what's done in the dark always comes to light.

Your character should drive how others perceive you.

Oftentimes we perceive ourselves one way but other people may view us another way. As long as you operate in integrity, what people see on the outside should never be too far from who you truly are on the inside. Think about it as building a house. If the foundation of the house is not properly set, the home cannot be built to its proper standards. Over time the home can develop cracks and potentially have even bigger problems due to the poor infrastructure. Alternatively, with a strong foundation the house can be built upon successfully from the ground up. Great leaders want to be surrounded by people with high integrity because they know that they can count on your solid foundation. Furthermore, in situations of high pressure they can count on you to do what is right. As you do right in the world you will always be abundantly blessed in return.

CHAPTER 16

Nothing in excess everything in moderation

I n the world we live in today everyone wants more and more and more. What they fail to realize is that less is more. You don't need anything in excess, only in moderation. As you begin to be successful don't forget where you started and how the simple things can bring you joy. Growing up one of my favorite after school snacks was a peanut butter and jelly sandwich. I would come home, turn on my favorite shows, and whip together a tasty peanut butter and jelly sandwich. Now, I enjoy dining at several well-known restaurants within the Tri-State area including my own. Yet still, I appreciate the comfort and simplicity of coming home after work and whipping together that world class peanut butter and jelly sandwich. While I fully enjoy the finer things, I know that they don't need to be consumed in excess. Don't forget the humbling things and where you started because too much of anything in excess is not good for you. We have seen stories of people eating in excess and becoming obese or sick. Additionally, we have seen and heard the news about people drinking alcohol or doing drugs and they end up causing serious harm to their health. I'm mindful of the portions of food I consume and conscious of eating too late in the evening. I like my food to be fully digested before going to sleep as it's better for my personal health. Additionally, I have moderate cocktails with friends or colleagues at networking events. Smoking cigarettes and vaping are also negative habits that consume the health as well as the finances of smokers. The dependency on a negative habit or product is not good. When you feel like you need something in excess, fast from it for a while to enhance your discipline.

Monitor your time spent on activities that do not add value to you because you don't have time to waste. You don't want to get to an age or point in your life where you say to yourself, "I wish I would have attempted to fulfill my dream." Stick to your goals and where you want to be in the future so you can look to achieve and accomplish them. Of course there will be some days where you want to do nothing but rest, even doing nothing should be done in moderation. Furthermore, spend your hard earned money wisely. Lastly, it's vital to do at least 30 minutes of physical activity per day. As you work out you will feel better, think wiser and as studies show you live longer.

CHAPTER 17

Form a foundation of financial literacy

In addition to your health, diet, and time management, moderation must also apply to your finances. As you begin to work in jobs, find your niche as a professional and begin to get paid for the work that you do, make sure to always pay yourself first. Pay all of your bills on time but don't forget to add yourself into those payments. This is called saving. It's always good to put money away for the future and potential investment opportunities. Circumstances can always change as you go through various seasons. You could potentially lose your job, have children, a family member can get sick, you never know the trials and tribulations life has in store for you. This ties back to always ensuring that you are prepared for whatever life may throw your way. When you're looking to make investment decisions, do your research and ensure you can get your full investment back in the first year. Make sure you believe in the business concept and the overall goal you're investing in. Once the investment is made, stay involved in the business and be aware of the latest developments.

It's also extremely important to build and maintain good credit. Credit is your financial reputation for handling loans in order for banks to determine if they can trust you with more loans. A loan from the bank can come in the form of credit cards, car loans, lines of credit, student loans, or mortgages. First and foremost, make timely payments which are at least more than the minimum required. Second, you don't want to have too much debt. Just because a bank approves you for a $10,000 loan, does not mean you need to take and spend $10,000 when you only needed $5,000 to begin with. Borrow according to your needs. Good credit will give you access to receiving future loans with lower interest rates and being approved for credit cards, cars and good rates on mortgages when you buy a home. Credit is extremely important to your financial success. Furthermore, when buying assets, purchase assets that appreciate (increase) in value such as real estate. Over time the value of the assets should make money for you, not lose money. A car is an asset that depreciates (decreases) in value. Also, clothing and jewelry often depreciate. Be cautious when selecting which items you want to buy and try not to make impulse purchases. A good rule of thumb is to wait 7-14 days before making a decision on a major purchase. If you can wait that long and you weigh the pros and cons of the item and you can soundly justify the purchase, then you know it is not an impulse buy. If it's a big purchase like a home, be patient, do your research and make sure it's right for you and fits into your future plans.

Warren Buffett is the CEO of Berkshire Hathaway, a philanthropist, and an investor. He is known as one of the richest people in the world. In spite of his substantial wealth, he lives a simple life. Although he has earned a lot of capital over his lucrative career, he still lives in the same house and drives the same car as he did decades ago. There are many lessons we can learn from billionaires like Warren who understand the importance of saving, leaving wealth for future generations, and giving back to the community. When you breakthrough in your finances, big or small, strive to keep your living expenses (overhead costs) low. A bonus or raise does not mean it is time for a shopping spree. It means you have more money to invest or set aside for a rainy day.

CHAPTER 18

Pack light and travel far for greater perspective

A s you are saving and investing, don't waste money on materialistic things but instead look for experiences that will create memories. An experience is a core component to an endless education that appreciates your value and elevates your brand while material things depreciate. Moments such as spending quality time with family and close friends make for the best memories. As a result, I travel to different countries a few times a year to relax, celebrate, meet new people and experience new cultures. The experiences are invaluable and memories are endless. Through traveling I get to change my atmosphere to reflect on where I am in life at the moment because pausing is necessary for peace of mind and to see the next steps ahead more clearly. Peace of mind is priceless. No amount of money, time or person should interfere with your peace. Refueling is essential. Think about it as if you are a car without gas. Eventually the car will shut down on the side of the road. Your life is a very similar concept. Humans are much more productive when we take a break and come back to a project or task with a fresh perspective, we become more effective in reaching the end goal. Vacation time allows us to take the time we need to recalibrate ourselves. Studies show that there are numerous benefits to taking a break from work including improved health, decreased stress, and increased motivation.

I look at traveling to different countries as one of my greatest achievements. I always strive to pack light and travel far. I pack light both mentally and physically. I never want to bring the weight of everything going on around me to another place. I leave the things creating stress behind in order to maximize the experience. As you pack light unconcerned with what is currently going on at home you'll be more susceptible to learn the culture you're engulfed in. Being inclusive to different countries, cultures and people is an amazing experience. We are all different which is the beauty between us. People speak various languages, eat unique foods, were raised differently, have diverse religions and all around experiences. With the increase in globalization within companies it's very important to continue learning different cultures. This can give you a competitive advantage when doing business or meeting with people from different countries. Most people appreciate when you know their culture and are pleased when you show a genuine interest and effort in trying to learn more about it. Consider traveling as a great opportunity to learn more about new people, places and yourself. We have to be respectful and inclusive of each other because that's how we will go further as people. Be patient though, you may not be able to travel tomorrow but with proper planning and exercising your financial literacy, you'll be able to have great experiences.

CHAPTER 19

Be patient greatness takes time

In your journey don't ever rush the process. I repeat, don't rush the process because patience is a virtue and greatness takes time. I always think of the saying "Rome wasn't built in a day". There have been many times where I wanted something to happen now — right now — instantly because that's the pace we live in today. Everything is instant whether it's buying something online, seeing pictures on social media or ordering food. Often when what I wanted to happen occurred later than I would have preferred, I would realize that I was much more prepared for the outcome. It simply never occurs when you want it to. It manifests when the time is right granted you stay the course. Timing is everything and when preparation, opportunity and timing come together you've reached the recipe for success.

Don't switch your passion or focus simply because you are being impatient. Make sure to stay in your lane and remain humble. Live with the expectation that the right opportunities will come your way. Hard work, focus, and determination can never be overlooked. As long as you're doing right and empowering others along the way, doors will open for you. Be patient though, it's not a sprint, it's a marathon. Maintain your own pace in order to withstand the longevity of the journey. I have run a few long distance races including the Corporate Challenge in Central Park. I always see the people that start the race at a steady, sustainable pace finish before the people who start off sprinting and later lose stamina. Similar to goals, it may take five to ten years for you to get one meeting that changes your entire business trajectory. No matter how long it takes, keep moving forward. Stay determined, consistent, and persistent because great things come in due time. As you make your way to the top of the building, don't forget to send the elevator back down for others. You are not truly successful until you help other people become successful as well.

CHAPTER 20

Lift as you levitate

As you turn into the leader I know you are and start to garner much success don't forget who you are and where you came from. This means you have to lift as you levitate. Each new phase of life means that there is someone else stepping into your previous phase. When you become a senior in high school preparing for life after school, there is a freshman who is starting their four year tenure. When you get a promotion at work, you have mastered the skills in your previous position to be able to mentor the person that just walked into that role. There are still people that you know and even some that you are yet to meet who are back where we began the journey of this book in Chapter 1. They are just coming to grips with the fact that they are the CEO of their own life and are taking that first step and they need your help getting their ideas off the ground. As you progress in each step of your journey you should be helping someone else progress along the way. That's where you will add meaningful value and leave a legacy of influence. I made the decision long ago that I don't want to be remembered as a man that only put himself in a better position. I must create opportunities for others because that is what I believe we are meant to do. Pay it forward.

I recently launched the Matthew C. Meade Scholarship Fund to provide economic resources for high school students to attend their dream college. Annually, I meet with the scholarship recipient and host a dinner party in their honor at my restaurant. I like to celebrate them and wish them luck as they pursue their college education. This is my way of planting a seed into their future, and that of my own, by giving back and helping others. Your legacy is defined by how many people you are able to impact in the world, not by how much money you have. A rich person buying a materialistic item doesn't hold as much value as a busy person giving their time to help others. Money makes solving certain problems easier but with money, problems still arise. I remember talking to one of the leaders at an investment bank about the progress I was making within the firm. He mentioned he'd been hearing great things about what I had been working on, but he quickly followed up the comment by asking, "Are you paying it forward?" I want you to ask yourself the same question about your recent success. Are you paying it forward? Who are you impacting and helping along the way?

Darkness and light cannot mix and it is your responsibility to be the light in every room you enter. Serve someone today, make them smile, and leave a long lasting impression. Every holiday season, my friends and I go to the train station in downtown Newark, New Jersey to feed the homeless. I'm honored to do it each year because the people we serve are so grateful and very much in need of what we are able to bring. We are blessed to be a blessing. You don't have to have a ton of resources to help someone. Do what you can with what you have. As you are helping others keep in mind that a good leader is defined by the leaders he or she creates. Put people in a position to be successful, create opportunities, break down doors and watch them soar. That too, will be a part of your legacy. There were plenty of people along your journey who paved the way, opened doors and believed in you. Be that person for the next trailblazer. While they are paving their way, remember to encourage them to blaze their own trail.

CHAPTER 21

Build a legacy that outlives you

N one of us will live in the physical form forever. While we are on our journey, it's vital to think about how we want to be remembered after our work here on Earth is done. What legacy do you want to leave behind for yourself? I think about this principle from time to time. I want to leave the world a better place than before I got here. I want to change lives, create opportunities and inspire others to be the best version of themselves. I truly push myself, family, and friends to be thought leaders and give back to the community. I don't want us to just live but instead to truly make an impact.

As we mature, get older and start having children it's never too early to start setting them up for success. We can do so by establishing a 529 College savings account for their education. Encourage and support them through extracurricular activities and teach good character traits of patience, discipline, focus, loyalty, honor, integrity and respect. These principles go a long way as children often follow your lead and learn from what they observe. Raising children, serving as a Godparent, teaching kids, or giving back to the community can all be a part of your legacy. Bring out the best in others and be a trailblazer. When people view you they should see hope and inspiration. A simple spark can ignite a fire. If you add fuel to the mix, the fire can grow even faster. For me, helping others, providing for future generations and making a community impact is a legacy that I am building that will outlive me.

I look at life as the test and the legacy left behind shows if you passed or failed. Through it all, finishing the test at the top of the class is a great achievement however you never want to forget why you are doing what you're doing in the first place. It's easy to detour off course and lose sight of the overall vision so don't get lost along your own path. Always keep at the forefront of your mind the reason why you started.

CHAPTER 22

Remember your why

Why? This is a question that all great leaders ask themselves over and over again. Why am I doing this? Why should I do this? Why does this matter? Why? Your *why* defines your purpose, your motive, and your passion. The journey is not always easy. There will be times when you're extremely tired. When you have everything to lose and nothing to gain, your why is what pushes you to keep going when you have no more stamina. It should be bigger than just you.

I wrote this book because I saw a need for a reference on the keys to life that will make you successful. I often look back at my high school and even middle school days and think about the essential components to being successful that were not taught in the classroom. I wanted to focus on what schools didn't teach and fill in the gaps that were missing. While the classroom provides you the basis for life skills and learning, experiences are the true playground for exploration. I speak to students in the Tri-State area during my free time because I know that if they had these principles they will have a head start in the real world. These 22 steps are near and dear to my heart because when I was starting out I didn't always know them and I had to learn them the hard way, through trial and error. Over the years I would have one-on-one conversations with young people and would be able to share some, but not all, of these best practices. I recognized the need for a road map to deliver. As a result, I wasn't able to sleep knowing I needed to get this information out to the world to help others. It wasn't easy. I had to weather the journey, not just the destination, by reflecting and really understanding what helped me the most. I often went back and changed or added principles because I wanted to share with you what was most effective to me over the years. There were times when I wanted to just get the book out to the people but kept it in my head because like I stated before it's not a sprint, it's a marathon. I knew that I wanted to deliver a genuine and authentic body of work that would help those of you who are reading this today by providing valuable wisdom.

If your why can be described in one word, what word would that be? For me the one word is "Impact". My goal has always been to love, help, teach and influence others to reach their full potential. When your why is big enough you will figure out your how. If there is something on your heart that you know you have to do but you keep procrastinating on it, think about the amount of people you can have a positive effect on when you achieve that goal. It shouldn't be just about you. Your why should always be bigger than you if you think about all the people who made sacrifices for your well being and to provide you an opportunity on Earth. You owe it to them — ancestors, forefathers, family — to be exceptional and impactul in all that you do. Most importantly, you owe it to yourself. Today is the day to navigate your road map swiftly and efficiently to be the leader that you were destined to be.

Go!

Made in the USA
Middletown, DE
29 August 2020

16822827R00036